THE CASE OF MRS. A

(The Diagnosis of a Life-Style)

by

DR. ALFRED ADLER

of Vienna

ALFRED ADLER INSTITUTE
PUBLISHERS
CHICAGO, ILLINOIS

INDIVIDUAL PSYCHOLOGY PUBLICATIONS

MEDICAL PAMPHLETS

Edited by

F. G. CROOKSHANK, M.D., F.R.C.P.

for the

Medical Society of Individual Psychology (London)

No. 1

First Published 1931

Reprinted 1969 by

ALFRED ADLER INSTITUTE

PUBLISHERS

CHICAGO, ILLINOIS

FIRST PUBLISHED IN ENGLAND
BY THE C. W. DANIEL CO., LTD.

Third Printing
ISBN #0-918560-00-4

EDITOR'S FOREWORD

INDIVIDUAL PSYCHOLOGY is the name given to a mode of thought, and examination of the human mind, devised by Dr. Adler, and developed by him, his friends and pupils, during the last twenty-five years. The name serves to distinguish that for which it stands from the Psycho-analysis of Freud and the Analytical Psychology of Jung.

It is true that all these three psychologies and methods are sometimes, by the public, included under the generic term *Psychoanalysis*. In one sense, this is rightly done, for they have much in common. That is to say, they are three modalities of the great psychological movement which, during the last thirty years, has swept away the old, formal, faculty and other psychologies of the nineteenth century, and which has done so much towards the freeing of mankind from the thrall of mere authoritarianism, and of oppressive taboos, exercised in restraint of happiness, and in satisfaction of meanness of soul, and a selfish will to power.

Yet it is essential that the specific distinctions indicated by the three names just given should be appreciated as keenly as is the generic bond. For the differences between the school of Adler, and those of Freud and of Jung, are not merely differences in therapeutic technique and analytic theory, to be glozed glibly by the slick verbiage of shallow eclectics.

No: they are differences of a fundamental kind, for each of the three great psychologies stands in a special relation to the principal subjects of metaphysical and philosophical controversy.

Thus, Individual Psychology differs from both Psycho-analysis and Analytical Psychology in taking up an attitude of healthy scepticism towards the ontological and epistemological discussions of verbalist contestants.

In respect of the scholastic controversy concerning the nature of *universals*—a controversy of perennial interest and basic importance —Individual Psychology, in full accord with the traditional empiricism of English thought, virtually adopts the conceptualism of William of Ockham, as revived in these latter days by Vaihinger.

Again, in the matter of causality, Individual Psychology stands very much where did Hume and Bentham, although, for the practical purposes of psychological investigation and psychotherapeutic effort, it stresses, at every moment, the notion of the *telos,* rather than that of the *eidos,* the *logos,* or the *morphe.*

To make use of a more familiar term, Individual Psychology, in the examination of psychical processes, regards always the "final cause," the *purpose* subserved, the *end* fulfilled. Thus, all psychic manifestations are considered AS IF willed, with an end in view; and there is, at the same time, a tendency growing from day to day to discuss even the somatic manifestations that we call signs or symptoms of disease as conditioned by their *meaning,* their *value* to the individual, the part they play in working out his scheme of life.

In this connection, it is necessary to mention the refusal of Individual Psychology to make the categorical distinction between mind and matter, mind and body, or *psyche* and *soma* so dear to those who, like the Freudians, seem to accept some kind of metaphysical dualism as satisfactory.

Individual Psychology settles the dispute as to the relation between *psyche* and *soma* by refusing to admit the *distinction* which is postulated by those who quarrel about the *relation.* It is concerned with the Individual alone, with the Unity, the Whole, and not with the component parts into which the Individual may be resolved, at the expense of losing his individuality, by ceasing to be that which he now is.

Individual Psychology settles also, for all practical purposes, the dispute between those who insist upon Freedom of the Will and those who are Determinists, or Predestinarians, by declaring the Individual to be personally and subjectively responsible for his own actions (so far as his endowment permits) at the same time that it admits the objective responsibility of the Family and of Society, for the fashion in which the demands of Life, to which the Individual must somehow or other respond, are presented to him, by them, during the formative years.

Individual Psychology recognizes, to the full, the part played in the formation of the *prototype* (or, character) during these early years by the response to the stimulus arising from the realisation of those qualities or dispositions we call *organ-inferiorities.* But Individual Psychology also teaches that, while the *subjective* realisation of these inferiorities taxes the individual *choice* of response— whether bravely, by effort; neurotically, by make-believe; or insanely, by retreat—the *objective* realisation of them should accentuate our feelings of responsibility, towards the child, for the manner in which those bigger and stronger than he make use of their strength and authority in relation to him.

Now there are three great demands that Life makes to the Individual, and they are those of Society, of Subsistence, and of Sex. Already from his day of issue from his mother's womb, the infant learns, at her breast, the need for that co-operation which lies at the basis of all social relations. Later, the father is responsible for the manner in which the problems and demands of occupation and subsistence are presented, but it is from the child's observation of the father-mother duplex that his first notions are formed of what the sexual relation may imply. Not always is this a notion of the reciprocal co-operation and mutual forbearance and aid that alone constitute an adequate foundation for successful adaptation to the sexual needs of Life.

"As the twig is bent, so is the tree inclined."

So, as the social, subsistence, and sexual problems are presented in childhood, and as the child responds thereto, so is the *life-style* formed, the *goal* chosen. So do we, as physicians, come to find, in the psychoses, the neuroses, and the somatoses of the periods of growth, maturity, and declination, clear manifestations of the failure of the Individual to have met one or other or all of these demands, having chosen wrongfully a life-style or goal, at the time of the formation of the prototype.

Now the neurotic failures in Life are found to be recruited from amongst: (i) those who are spoilt, or, in Adler's phraseology, are "pampered" and; (ii) those who are snubbed. Whether a child be spoilt or snubbed, in either case his sense of capacity, of independence, is thwarted. No less is this true when (iii) there is consciousness of a crippling or weakening "organ-inferiority." But to be spoilt, pampered, snubbed, discouraged, frightened, or browbeaten is, in itself, to make a wrong response to circumstance. However hard, even inexcusably hard, may be the situation, there is never any warrant for individual failure at least to attempt a suitable response, and it is axiomatic for Individual Psychology that "Every human being can do everything." As Dr. Béran Wolfe has said, with the greatest point, in his preface to Dr. Adler's *The Pattern of Life* (1931): "To treat a child AS IF he could adjust himself to the scheme of society costs nothing, and often accomplishes miracles."

So the ultimate neurotic failure is the child who has not, in his early days, either prepared or been prepared for Life: who has not learned to combine the exercise of a manly independence or self-reliance with the practice, for social and not selfish reasons, of that co-operation which safeguards the individual himself, at the same time that he contributes to the security of others. And so doctors, who have to cope with the "neurotic failures," have come to find in Individual Psychology not only a philosophy of life, not only a method of education, but an actual and active psychotherapy. That is to say, it teaches us how to adjust, how to "get well," how to become "whole"—for health and whole-th mean the same thing—

and, by the same token, how to become happy and useful members of society.

Thus regarded, Individual Psychology is seen to be of the greatest importance to all medical men: physicians, practitioners and psychologists. Clinically, it has proved its worth a thousand times. But the proof is not to be found in tendencious statistical tables: rather is it established by the daily lives of those who have grasped its principles, and by the unparalleled spread of its influence, in the last few years, in Europe and in America. True, in England, this influence is to the superficial observer less obvious than elsewhere. Nevertheless, Individual Psychology is now permeating British Medicine and Sociology in a fashion that is easily recognized by those who are acquainted with Dr. Adler's writings.

No doubt the Academicals of the Established Teaching Hospitals, deeply engrossed in the mnemonics of the lecture-room, the technique of the operating-theatre, and the researches of the deadhouse and the pathological laboratory, continue to ignore—or so it seems—the relevancy of a study of Human Nature to the practice of Medicine. But is not *Ichabod* already written, for those who have eyes to see, over the portals through which still pass not a few "neurotic failures" on their melancholy progress to be deprived *seriatim* of one organ after another, at the bidding of surgeons to whom even the diagnosis of "Nothing organic: *only* functional" is as a counsel of despair?

However, nothing is more striking than the manner in which, during the last year or two, our native psychotherapists, even without nominal acknowledgment and in spite of their professed allegiance in other quarters—or, may be, their ostentatious eclecticism—have come to adopt the thought and practice connected with the name of Alfred Adler. Indeed, to borrow a turn of phrase from the late Sir William Harcourt; "We are all Individual Psychologists now." But, even if popular identification of the Teacher with the Teachings is still lacking, there are, in London at least, two groups of Individual Psychologists, working with real and increasing success.

It is on behalf of one of these groups, or Societies—the Medical Society of Individual Psychology, with a meeting-place at 11 Chandos Street, Cavendish Square—that the present pamphlet—it is hoped, the first of perhaps many periodical publications—has been issued. This Society, as its name implies, is a purely medical one. The other group of which mention has been made—the London Branch of the International Society of Individual Psychology—has a wider aim, and embraces men and women who are not, as well as those who are, medical practitioners amongst its members. At present, the headquarters are at 55 Gower Street and the honorary secretary is Mrs. Stephen Graham.

FOREWORD

In this connection, it may not be irrelevant to remark that the study of the philosophical, sociological, educational and other bases and implications of Individual Psychology cannot possibly be ignored. For Individual Psychology is no closed doctrinal system, but rather a method of very wide application. And, without going too far, it may be said that Einstein's own interest in Adler's work and thought warrants the suggestion that, in Individual Psychology we have an application, within the psychological frame of reference, of the general principle of Relativity itself.

But a few words are necessary to explain the circumstances of the publication of this pamphlet.

In January 1931, Dr. Adler himself visited London and gave a series of lectures on various aspects of Individual Psychology, under the joint auspices of the two societies already mentioned.

One address was actually delivered before the Psychiatric Section of the Royal Society of Medicine, and another before the Medical Section of the British Psychological Society. (Good reports were given in the *Lancet,* January 17 and 31, 1931, and the *British Medical Journal,* January 24, 1931.) But, on the occasion of a special meeting, at the rooms of the MEDICAL SOCIETY OF INDIVIDUAL PSYCHOLOGY, it was felt that a demonstration, by Dr. Adler, of his own methods of reading a "life-style" would be of the greatest interest. It was therefore arranged, at Dr. Adler's own request, that, at the last moment, case-notes made by a practising physician should be presented to him for his extempore consideration and impromptu interpretation.

To this end, Dr. Hilda Weber was good enough to transcribe, and bring to the meeting, notes taken by her, some time previously, on the case of one "Mrs. A" who had been under her care. The nature of the case was known to no one other than Dr. Weber until the moment when the notes were handed to Dr. Adler on the platform, after the fashion of what undergraduate examinees call an "unseen"! It is perhaps right to say that Dr. Weber, when these notes were first taken down, was not personally interested in Individual Psychology, while it is certain that no alteration was made in them for the purposes of the meeting.

This statement is made with particularity, in order that the commentary made by Dr. Adler can be properly appreciated. Moreover, it throws into strong relief the truth that the inferences and judgments of the Individual Psychologist are ever closely approached by the candid and commonsense observer without doctrinal prejudices.

In this context a true story may be told. During a recent visit to America, Dr. Adler was asked by an eminent physician why he (Dr. Adler) called himself a psychologist when he "only spoke common-sense." To which the pertinent reply was made: "But why then do you not also?"

In preparing for publication the verbatim notes taken by Miss Margaret Watson of Dr. Adler's demonstration, Dr. Adler's own words have been allowed to stand practically as uttered. Only the absolute minimum of alteration necessary to secure understanding was made, for it was felt, not only that all suspicion of editing should be avoided, but that any attempt at stylistic or syntactical emendation would destroy at once the charm and the essential lucidity of the spoken word. For, as a matter of fact, in so much that Dr. Adler has said and written *in his own way* his meaning has thus been better conveyed than it otherwise could have been. Few writers and speakers have suffered more at the hands of translators and editors. If we try to understand what Dr. Adler thinks and means, whether he is addressing us in his native tongue, or in our own, we succeed more perfectly than if we undertake a verbal or grammatical analysis. We come thus best to appreciate the stark significance of some of his aphorisms and judgments, even when they seem to some of his critics most simple and commonplace, or even banal.

But the Individual Psychologist who, like William of Ockham, understands the true function of words as a vehicle for thought, is not likely to fall into the superficial error of confounding the medium with what is transmitted. Perhaps it is through failure to appreciate this true function of words that Individual Psychology has been reproached with obviousness—as if simplicity and directness *should* be a reproach!—by some of those who, as Adler says "esteem highly words."

Perhaps, too some of those who make Individual Psychology the object of their scorn, have been apt, when gazing into the Well, to mistake their own surface-reflection for that ultimate Truth which we are not ashamed to believe lies couched more deeply in its tenebrous profundity.

F.G.C.

FOREWORD TO SECOND EDITION

Beginning in 1931 and continuing until the war years interrupted such activity in England, the Medical Society of Individual Psychology in London produced a series of "Medical Pamphlets" which were published by the C. W. Daniel Company. Their value was uneven, their topics ranged far and wide. Some of the contents were only remotely connected to Individual Psychology. The first such pamphlet consisted of verbatim notes of a demonstration by Adler of his method of understanding a life style from reading a case history. The "reading" was presented entire and a foreword was written by Crookshank, one of the founders and prime movers behind the London Society.

Crookshank's depth of understanding of Individual Psychology is shown in his foreword, which actually reviews the basic principles of I. P. His sympathetic editing hand left the words of Adler mainly intact and for this reason the work assumes importance for us as a demonstration of a diagnostic *method* used by Adlerians.

Individual Psychologists have devised a large variety of diagnostic techniques, but one of their oldest techniques is the one herein used by Adler: the diagnosis of a life style by a "reading" of a case history. Adler does more than induce a life style, he interprets for us a whole psychological picture of the personality, including its development and deduces various clusters of behavioral traits that the person may be expected to display. Throughout, Adler shows how he picks up a theme that runs through the history, juggles other facts until they fit in with the theme and make an organized whole.

The faculty of the Alfred Adler Institute of Chicago decided to reprint *The Case of Mrs. A* because they wanted it to be readily available to students at the Institute. The pamphlet has been required reading in the course on Diagnosis, but the small number of copies available discouraged its use. The present editor has tried to make the pamphlet even more useful by explaining and elaborating where such seems required.

BHS.
1968

THE CASE OF MRS. A

I HAVE first to thank you all for your attention and for your eagerness to look into the workroom of Individual Psychology. My purpose is to approach it in this way: As you are partly trained and accustomed as doctors, I asked to receive an analysis of a sick, neurotic or psychotic person, knowing nothing about it. So you see this really is a clinic and you know what you have to do. You have to use general diagnosis and special diagnosis and so on. So you see we are in the general field of medicine. We do not act in any other way. We know that in general medicine we have to use all our means, all our tools, because otherwise we would not feel justified in going on to therapy. Now in this case we have to deal with mental conditions and so we must have an idea, a conception of mind. We are looking for mind as for a part of life. I do not believe we can go further. We do not know more, but we are satisfied, because we see that in other sciences also they cannot explain more. What are electricity, gravitation and so on? Probably for a long time, or for ever, nobody can contribute any more to our knowledge of mind than that it is a faculty of life, a part of life. Therefore, if life can be understood we shall find that mind also wants to grow up and develop towards an ideal final goal. This means that we have to consider at least two points.

One is the point from which the symptom expression takes its rise. We shall find that wherever we can lay our finger on a complaint there will be a lack, the feeling of a *minus*. And mind always wants to overcome this *minus*, and strive for an ideal final form. We say that wherever there is life there is a striving for an ideal final form. I cannot explain today all the finer features and characteristics of this growing up. It is enough if I remind you that in Individual

Psychology we are looking for the situation in which a person feels confronted, and does not feel able to overcome a certain problem or difficulty. *Therefore, we have to look for the direction in which such a person is striving.*

In this direction we meet with a million varieties, and these varieties can be measured to a certain degree if we have an idea of what *co-operation* means, and *social interest*. Very often we are able to calculate how far away from a right degree of co-operation we find this kind of patient striving. Therefore it is necessary—and each good analysis has to bring it about—to find on which point a person proves not to be prepared rightly for the solution of social problems, not to be prepared rightly because he cannot afford what is expected of him, the right degree of courage, of self-confidence, of social adjustment, the right type of co-operation and so on. These things must be understood because you will see how the patient cannot *pay*, how he declares himself not to be able to solve his problem and how he shows what I call the *hesitating* attitude, the *stopping* attitude. He begins to *evade* and wants to secure himself against a solution of the necessary problem.

On this point you will find him in the state of mind I have described as the Inferiority Complex.[1] and, because of that, he is always striving to go ahead, to feel superior, to feel that he has overcome his difficulties in the present situation. You must look for this point where the patient *feels* satisfied on account of *feeling* superior. Now he cannot feel superior in regard to the solution of his present problem in a useful way and therefore his superiority is proved in the line of uselessness. In his own imagination he has reached his goal of superiority and perhaps satisfied himself, but it cannot be valued as a goal of usefulness.

---

[1] In his later years, Adler used the terms "Inferiority Complex" to describe a state of mind in which the person is impressed by a defect in himself. We prefer to use the term "inferiority feeling" to describe this state of felt deficiency and to reserve "inferiority complex" for those situations where the person uses the deficiency as an *excuse* for avoiding finding a solution to the problem.

THE DIAGNOSIS OF A LIFE-STYLE

This is the first description we would expect in each case history, in each analysis of a mental case; it belongs to the GENERAL DIAGNOSIS. Again belonging to the general diagnosis, we have to find some explanation of *why* this person has not been prepared. This is difficult to understand and to recognise. We have to delve back into the past of this person, to find out in what circumstances he has grown up, how he has behaved towards his family and to ask questions resembling very much the questions we ask in general medicine. We ask: "What were your parents like?" The patients do not know that in their answers they express their whole attitude—if they felt pampered, and the centre of attention, or if they resented one or the other of their parents—but *we* see it. And especially on this point always give "empty" questions! You will then be sure that you do not insinuate and give a hint to the patient to speak as you want him to speak.

At this point you will see the origin of the lack of preparation for the present situation which is like a test examination. *Why* the patient has not been prepared for it must be seen and explained in the case history.

That is the GENERAL DIAGNOSIS,[2] but you must not believe that when you have done this you have understood the patient. Now begins the SPECIAL DIAGNOSIS.[3] In the SPECIAL

---

[2] General Diagnosis thus includes:
 1. What produces the feeling of deficiency (the critical problem).
 2. The direction in which the person strives to overcome the perceived deficiency.
 3. The relationship of the direction of striving to the "right degree of cooperation."
 4. The point on which the person is not prepared rightly for the solution of social problems (lack of preparation in courage, confidence, social adjustment, cooperation)
 5. The way in which the person shows the hesitating attitude and evades the problem.
 6. The way in which the person arranges to feel superior even though he is avoiding the problem.
 7. What in the past history explains why the person has been improperly prepared for life.

[3] By Special Diagnosis Adler seems simply to mean the finding of corroborative evidence.

DIAGNOSIS you must learn by testing. It is the same kind of testing as you need, for example, in internal medicine. You must note what the patient says but, as in general medicine, you must not trust yourself. You must prove it, and not believe, if you find, for example, a certain frequency of the palpitations of the heart, that it necessarily means a particular cause. In medicine and surgery, as in Individual Psychology, you have to guess,[4] but you have to prove it by other signs which agree, and if you have guessed and *they* do not agree, you have to be hard and cruel enough against yourself to look for another explanation. What I want to do today is to take an analysis such as we might have in a clinic, for example. The doctor makes an analysis of a patient he has not seen before and tries to explain. We, perhaps, may work in this way, for then the whole audience is forced, willingly or unwillingly, to think it over.

Individual Psychology expects you to prove every rule. You must reject each rule and try to *understand* and at last you will feel justified in your general views. Of course, you

---

[4] *Guessing* is stressed by Adler as an important diagnostic method. "To give an orientation to one's observations, which include the patient's symptoms, experiences, manner of life and development, I use three devices. The first assumes that the life-plan originated under aggravated conditions, such as organ inferiorities, pressure in the family, pampering, rivalry or a neurotic family tradition and directs my attention to childhood reactions similar to the present symptoms. The second device assumes the personality ideal is the determining factor of the neurosis. The third device looks for the largest common denominator for all accessible expressive movements. Until recent times it was chiefly the poets who best succeeded in getting the clue to a person's style of life. . . . This power was due to their gift of divination. Only by guessing did they come to see what lies behind and between the expressive movements, namely the individual's law of movement (from *The Individual Psychology of Alfred Adler*, edited by Ansbacher, H&R, New York, Basic Books, 1956. pp. 328-329).

All guesses are therefore within the framework for understanding behavior that Adler described. Dreikurs also points out that the "guessing" is not random—"One does not need to rely on intuition and vague impressions to 'sense' the patient's inner logic, if one is trained to observe human actions as movements toward (in relation to) others and life, if the ability to recognize and analyze purposive behavior has been fostered and systematically developed." (Psychodynamics, Psycho-therapy and Counseling. Collected Papers. Chicago: Alfred Adler Institute, 1967. p. 271).

cannot help being influenced in your enquiries by those general views, but it is the same as in other sciences and especially in Medicine. You must get rid of your understanding, for instance, of period, of constitution, of the work of the endocrine glands, and so on. But it is very worth while, because you have a hint, and you can go on what you find in this way. It is really the result of your thinking and shows whether you are thinking rightly or not, if you are experienced or not, and so on. It is the same with Individual Psychology and, therefore, so far as I can see, Individual Psychology agrees wholly with the fundamental views of Medicine.[5]

Now here is the case of Mrs. A. What we can see is that she is a married woman—perhaps a widow—we do not know more. You must fix each word and turn it over in your mind so that you may get everything that is in it.

> *The patient A who forms the subject of this paper, was 31 years old at the time she came for treatment.*

Thirty-one years old and a married woman! Now we know circumstances in which a woman, thirty-one years old, and married, might find herself. There could be a problem of marriage, of children, perhaps also a problem of income in these times. We are very careful. We would not pre-suppose anything, but we feel sure that—unless we are surprised later—there is something wrong in one of these ways. Now we go ahead.

> *She had been married eight years...*

That carries us further—she had married at twenty-three years of age.

> *... and had two children, both boys, aged eight and four years respectively.*

---

[5] Adler correctly points out that the diagnostic procedure he is suggesting is similar to the approach a physician uses to a diagnostic problem; namely, to collect data, conjecture and test the conjectures until a fit is found.

Now she had a child very soon. Eight years married and the child eight years old! What you think about that is your own affair. Perhaps we have to correct an anamnesia. You see the sharp eye of Individual Psychology!

> *Her husband was a lift man in a Stores.*

Then they are probably in poor circumstances.

> *An ambitious man, he suffered considerable humiliation from the fact that, unlike his brother, he was prevented, he felt, from obtaining a better type of employment because during the war his right arm had been disabled.*

If we can trust this description that he is an ambitious man and does not feel happy in his employment, this must reflect in his married life. He cannot satisfy his ambition outside the family. Perhaps he tries to satisfy it inside; tries to rule his wife and children and to "boss" them. We are not sure and we must be careful enough not to believe it and to be convinced, but we have a view. Perhaps we shall find something in this way. An ambitious husband!

> *His wife, however, had little sympathy with his trouble, ...*

Now if we are right that this man wants to prove himself superior in his family life and his wife does not agree and give in, if she has little sympathy with his style of life, there must probably be some dissension in the family. This man wants to rule; his wife does not agree and does not give him a chance. Therefore, there must be trouble in the family.

> *... being far too occupied with the compulsive thoughts and fears of death from which she suffered.*

Compulsive thoughts and fear of death! It does not look like a compulsion neurosis; it looks more like an anxiety neurosis. Now on this point I should like to give you a rule out of our experience which can be used. I like to ask: what happens in these cases? What are the results if a married woman is suffering from fears of death and perhaps from other fears? What would it mean?[6] She is occupied too much with it, as we can see, and so many of her necessary tasks would not be fulfilled. We see that she is much more occupied with her own person. She is not interested, as we have heard, in the troubles of the man.

We are, therefore, in agreement on these points, but we are not far ahead. We can understand that such a person cannot co-operate rightly if she is interested in the fear of death and other fears, and we understand that there must be many dissensions in this family.

> *These fears, indeed, occupied her mind to such an extent that she found difficulty at the time she came for treatment in thinking of anything else.*

At this point we are justified in answering our question: what happens? She cannot think of anything else.[7] Now I want to tell you that this is what you will always find and, if in any cases it appears not to be so for a time, you will find confirmation later in the description. This shows that it is worth while, and encourages us because we know we are not right off the mark but have predicted what will be later.

We read that she is thinking only of her fears.

> *Thus a careful housewife—she had previously been governed by an almost obsessional hatred of dirt and love of tidiness, . . .*

---

[6] Here is Adler's teleological point of view at work. In order to understand the meaning of the symptom, one asks what is its purpose? What is it unconsciously intended to accomplish? Techniques for determining the actual purpose of a symptom have been described by Dreikurs, R. (Psycho-dynamic diagnosis in psychiatry. Amer. of Psychiatry, 1963, 119, 1045-1048) and various purposes of symptoms have been described by Shulman, B. H. and Mosak, H. H. (Various purposes of symptoms. Journal of Indiv. Psychol. 1967, 23, 79-87) Wolfe, W. B. (Nervous Breakdown, London: Routledge and KeganPaul, 1934 Chap. 2, pp. 38-62) and by Adler himself (The Individual Psychology of Alfred Adler edited by Ansbacher, H. L. and Ansbacher, R. R. New York: Basic Books, 1956, pp. 263-280).

[7] Adler here takes a key statement from the history which describes "the consequence" of the symptoms and which reveals the purpose. His prediction was correct.

This gives another picture—a compulsion neurosis in regard to cleanliness, probably a wash-compulsion neurosis.[8] If she was afraid of dirt she must make it clean always. She must wash and clean everything and herself. In the same way she is suffering from fear of death. There must be a mixed neurosis. This is really very rare. In our general experience the wash-compulsion neurotics do not suffer from fear of death. They may combine the two ideas and say: "If I do not wash his desk, or these shoes and so on, my husband will die," or whatever it may be. But that is not the fear of death as we find it in many anxiety neuroses. As I explained in a lecture in this room on "Obsessions and Compulsion in the Compulsion Neuroses" there is always an underlying idea. Here the idea is that of cleaning away the dirt.

Now we understand more on this point. We see that this woman is occupied in another place than that in which she is expected to be. She does not co-operate, she is interested only in her own sufferings, making everything clean and perhaps, the wash-compulsion. Therefore, we can judge: this is a type that can solve the social problems of life, but she is not prepared in co-operation but much more prepared in thinking of herself. We know out of our general experience that we find such a style of life mostly in children suffering from imperfect organs, in the great majority pampered, petted and dependent children. More rarely we find it in neglected children, because probably a child wholly neglected would die. The great majority of these neurotic children have been pampered, made dependent and given such an idea of themselves that they are more interested in themselves than in others.

---

[8] Adler is guessing that a compulsive neurosis has been present. In line with his subsequent statements, it is also our experience that a washing-compulsion neurosis is not generally "mixed" with an anxiety reaction, but anxiety reactions are frequently found in people with obsessive characters. The common denominator is the desire of the person to "control" what happens around him. See Mosak, H. H. "The Interrelatedness of the Neuroses Through Central Themes." J. of Indiv. Psychol., 1968, 24, 67-70.

Actually, there was no washing compulsion in this case, but plenty of obsessive symptoms.

THE DIAGNOSIS OF A LIFE-STYLE 19

This woman is striving for a high ideal—to be cleaner than all the others. You can understand that she does not agree with our life; she wants it to be much cleaner. Now cleanliness is a very nice characteristic and we like it very much but if a person focuses life on cleanliness she is not able to live our life, and there must be another place for such a person, because if you have really enquired into cases of wash-compulsion neurosis, you will be convinced that it is not possible to arrive at such an ideal of cleanliness as these people want to arrive at. You will always find *some* dirt and dust. You cannot carry on life by pointing to *one* part only —cleanliness, for instance— because it disturbs the harmony of life.

So far as I can see there is only one part of our emotions and life that can never be overstrained and that is *social interest*. If there is *social interest* you cannot overstrain it in such a degree that the harmony of life can be disturbed, but all other things can do so. If you point to health and think only of it, you ruin your life; if you think only of money, you ruin your life, in spite of the fact that, as we know, it is unfortunately necessary to think of it. If you turn to family life and exclude all the other relations, you ruin your life. It seems an unwritten law that we cannot turn only to one point without risking many damages!

Now we will see more.

> .... *hatred of dirt and love of tidiness, both with regard to her home and to her own person—she now began to show neglect in both these particulars.*

This also is not usual, for we mostly receive such persons, with their care for cleanliness and avoidance of dirt, in this frame of mind. But this woman has broken down, so she gives up. We do not know how she appears now in this state of mind, but it is very probable that she did not succeed in her imagination with this compulsion neurosis and, therefore, she has made one step forward, coming—if I have read and understood rightly—to a state in which she begins to neglect herself and to be dirty.

Now here is an interesting point. I have never seen persons so dirty as those suffering from a wash-compulsion neurosis. If you enter the home of such a person there is a terrible fume. You find papers lying about, and dirt everywhere. The hands and the whole body are dirty, all the clothes are dirty and they do not touch anything. I do not know if it is so here, but this is the usual condition among people with a wash-compulsion neurosis and it is funny that all these persons experience some adventures that others never experience. Always, where there is dirt, they are mixed in it. Probably it is because they are always looking round for dirt and are not so clever as others in avoiding it. I have had a very queer experience with such persons who are always soiled where other people can avoid it. It is like a fate hanging over such people, that they must always find their way to dirt.

We do not know what the breakdown means in this case —perhaps a step nearer to psychosis.[9] That happens sometimes in persons suffering from compulsion neurosis.

Her fear of death referred to above was related to a definite knife phobia—

You can call a knife phobia also a compulsion idea,[10] a very frequent one which persons suffer from if they see a knife. They feel that they could kill a person. But they never do. They stop at the idea. The meaning behind such an idea is hidden; we must find out its whole coherence and what it means. Now I have explained what it means. It is nearly the same as a person wanting to curse—"I could kill you," and such things.

We spoke before of dissensions. The husband is ambitious. She, as we know from our general diagnosis of neurotic persons, is ambitious. She wants to rule, to be the

---

[9] Here Adler overlooks the concept that the anxiety reaction itself may temporarily remove the need to use compulsive cleanliness and order as a control device. According to the Law of Parsimony, the compulsive cleanliness will not be used if the anxiety reaction achieves the desired goals. Had the cleanliness continued to achieve the goals, no anxiety reaction would have occurred.

[10] Today we would call it an "obsessive thought."

head.[11] She wants to be the cleanest person, and we can understand how she avoids her husband, his personal approach, his sexual approach, because of his lack of cleanliness. She calls everything dirty. She can call a kiss dirt.[12] We cannot commend her. We must find how far she is going to look for this dirt. She has two children and we must believe that this had not been at her own wish. Here we see the lack of co-operation. If you look a little nearer you may be sure this is a frigid woman. Do you see why? She is always thinking of herself, and the sexual functions among men and women can be right *only if they are fulfilled as a task for two persons.* If a person is interested only in self the sexual feelings are not right. Thus you have frigidity. More rarely you may have vaginismus, but it is mostly frigidity, and you can be sure that this is a woman who does not co-operate. This can be seen in the *form* of her sexual urge, which is *sexuality*. We must remember the difference—sexuality is a *form* [13] and sexual urge is a *movement*. Therefore we can be sure and can predict—though we must not allow ourself to do so, but should wait and be patient—that she resents sexual intercourse.

We next read that this knife phobia was

> ... connected with tendencies both suicidal and homicidal.

In the discussion of suicide, I have explained that this is always a sign of a person who is not trained in co-operation. He is always looking after himself, and when he is confronted with a social problem for which he is not prepared, he has such a feeling of his own worth and value that he is

---

[11] Adler surmises this but has not yet proved it.

[12] Adler is describing traits found in a compulsively clean wife where she is annoyed with her husband. He is guessing that the wife is angry at the husband. He mentions the distaste for sex and pregnancy that is usually seen in such people.

[13] This is an Adlerian epistemological concept. All feelings (sexual urge) are understood as movements. Sex itself is a *medium* through which the movement occurs. The word *medium* is perhaps more descriptive than *form* (e.g. a *"medium* of expression").

sure that, in killing himself, he hurts another person. If you have seen such cases in this connexion, you have understood them. Therefore we can say in a certain way that suicide is always an accusation and a revenge, an attacking attitude.[14] Sometimes it is an attack of revenge. Therefore, we must look for the person against whom this phobia is directed. There is no question that it is her husband. It may be guessed very surely—the husband with whom as we have seen, she must be in dissension. He wants to rule and she is interested only in her own person, and therefore if there is revenge or attack or aggression against somebody, it must be against the husband. You can guess it, but please wait to see if we can prove it.

> *Her aggressive thoughts and feelings towards other people were shown in other ways.*

We see "other people." We do not know who they are, but it contradicts in a certain way our view that the husband is meant.

> *She experienced at times an impulsive wish to hit her husband...*

That is what I said before. It is as in general medicine. If you have guessed before, you may find a proof. If you have rapidly diagnosed pneumonia for instance, you may find signs later that will prove it and which you can predict; when we find such proofs we feel that we are on terra firma.

> *...her husband or...*

We know what must follow—her husband or the children. There are no other persons she could accuse. She would not like children. If you asked her: "Do you like children?" she would say "Yes: my children are my all!" In Individual

---

[14] For further discussion of this point see Adler, Kurt A. "Depression in the Light of Individual Psychology" J. of Indiv. Psychol., 1961 17, 56-67 and Karon, B. "Suicidal Tendency as the Wish to Hurt Someone Else and Resulting Treatment Technique," ibid, 1964, 20, 206-212.

Psychology we learn from experience that if we want to understand a person we have to close our ears. We have only to look. In this way we can see as in a pantomime. Perhaps there are other persons. Perhaps there is a mother-in-law. It is possible. We would not be astonished. But, so far as we know the situation, we expect the children to follow.

> . . . her husband or anybody else who happened to have annoyed her.

Who are the persons who can have annoyed her? We can see that this woman is very sensitive and if we look for what sensitiveness means in general diagnosis we find that it means a feeling of being in a hostile country and being attacked from all sides.[15] That is the style of life of the person who does not co-operate and feel at home, who is always experiencing and sensing enmity in the environment and, therefore, we can understand that she reacts in such a strong manner with emotion.

If I felt I was in a hostile country and always expected attacks, expected to be annoyed and humiliated, I would behave in the same way. I also would be a sensitive. This is a very interesting point. We cannot explain these persons only by looking to their emotion; we must look to their mistaken meaning of life and to their bringing up. She really believes she lives in a hostile country and is expecting always to be attacked and humiliated. She is thinking only of herself and her own salvation, her own superiority in overcoming the difficulties of life. These emotional persons must be understood from this point of view. If I believe an abyss is before me, whether there is an abyss or not, it is all the same; I am suffering from my meaning, not from reality. If I believe that there is a lion in the next room, it is all the same to me whether there is one or not. I shall behave in the

---

[15] We now use the term "oversensitive" to describe the person who reacts with emotional distress to any unpleasantness or opposition. Being oversensitive is a passive covert way of being antagonistic and oppositional. It is often a polite substitute for anger, as when a person denies anger saying, "I wasn't angry, I was *hurt*."

same way.[16] Therefore, we must look for the meaning of this person. It is "I must be safe"—a selfish meaning.

Now we read:

> These characteristics had of late extended in two directions. On the one hand she experienced at times a strong desire to hit any casual stranger she happened to pass in the street.

Is it not as I have described? She is living in a hostile country, where everybody is an enemy. To want to hit any stranger she meets in the street means to be impossible, to compromise herself. It means: "I must be watched: someone must take care of me." She forces other persons—or one other person—to take care of her. Whether she says it in words or not she speaks by her attitude in life and forces other persons to take care of her if she behaves in this way. But we must also look for the impression the husband has of it. His wife wants to hit every stranger in the street and he is living with her in social relations. Therefore, whatever she does affects him. He must do something. What can he do in such a case? We suppose this husband is not a fool or feebleminded and we can predict what he has to do. He has to take care of her as far as possible, watch her and accompany her and so on. She is giving him the rules for his behaviour in so doing. You see this ambitious woman with an ambitious husband has conquered. He must do what she wants and commands. She behaves in such a way that other persons must feel responsible. She exploits him and is the commander and, therefore, we can understand that on this point, she rules.

Now let us see more:

> On the other hand she entertained homicidal feelings towards her younger son, a child of four...

This we have not seen before, but we have guessed it—that the attacks would be against the children. Here we

---

[16] Here Adler begins to describe how a basic attitude leads to a cluster of behavioral traits.

have the second child specially pointed out, and it gives us a chance to guess that she wanted to avoid this child, that it was an unwanted child and it finds expression in this way that she is afraid she will kill him, that she does not treat him rightly and so on. These feelings are sometimes so intense that the husband must watch her. The husband now becomes a slave and probably this woman had nothing more in her meaning and imagination long ago, but to make him a prisoner and slave. She would have been satisfied if her husband had submitted in a general way, as sometimes husbands do submit. But we have heard that this husband was ambitious; he wanted her to submit, wanted to subjugate her. He has lost and she has conquered. She could not conquer in a usual way, convincing him, or perhaps taking part in all his interests, therefore she came to a point that we can understand. She is right; she acts intelligently. If her goal is to be conqueror, to subjugate her husband, she has acted absolutely rightly. She has accomplished a creative work, a masterpiece of art, and we have to admire this woman!

Now I want to tell you something of how I go on with such cases. I explain it in short words. I say: "I admire you; you have done a masterpiece of art. You have conquered." I put it pleasantly.[17]

Now we want to establish a coherence. This woman is looking for a fear that she will kill somebody. We have to look for the whole coherence. She is leaning on one point and is not looking for the others. Other psychologists will say she is surprised, but she is not surprised.[18] I see it clearly.

---

[17] This is a typically Adlerian way of making an interpretation. Instead of making an inflammatory accusing statement, Adler makes an ironic statement which commends the cleverness of the patient and her success in achieving her private goal. The patient does not expect such a commendation. She may react with a smile of recognition (recognition reflex) or may deny the validity of the interpretation or may change the subject and claim she is only tortured by the symptoms and wants to get rid of them. Nevertheless, the therapist will have presented an alternate way of looking at the symptoms and hopefully, opened an avenue of discussion.

[18] Probably meaning that she already "knows" in some sense that her goal is to conquer. This type of "knowing" fits the Adlerian explanation of the unconscious as that which is unattended to; but also will fit the Freudian idea of repressed wish.

She does not want to see it, because, if she did, her remainder of social interest would rise up and contradict it. No person who is not feeble-minded or crazy would agree that he wanted to rule other persons in such a way and, therefore, she is not permitted to look. But we must make her look and, therefore, I prefer to have such a nice talk and to praise her for her cleverness: "You have done rightly."

Then there is the question whether, even before she had no other meaning or goal in her mind but to rule everybody. On this point we have to find out whether in childhood also she was "bossing" and wanted to command everybody.[19] If we can prove it as the next backward step in our understanding what shall we say of all the scepticism, all the criticisms that we do not know anything about this woman and how she was as a child? If we can show that as a child she was "bossing," in what other science can you be so sure that you can postulate something which happened twenty-five or twenty-eight years before? If you ask her for her earliest recollections, I am sure she will tell you something in which you will find a "bossing" attitude, because we are soon to grasp the whole style of life of this woman. She is a "bossing" woman, but she could not conquer in a normal way. She had no chance—poverty, an ambitious husband, two children very soon, not co-operative, as we have seen. She had to be defeated in a normal way and she is looking for her conquest in another way that we could not agree with or call a useful or social way.

> *Sometimes the idea of killing the boy was so intense that she feared that she might carry the intention into execution.*

The more she was afraid she would execute it, the more her husband must watch her.

> *She stated that these symptoms had been in existence for one and a half years.*

---

[19] Now Adler will look for further evidence in the person's childhood in his attempt to establish a life style for the person (point 7 of the General Diagnosis). Unfortunately, no earliest childhood recollections were given in this history.

If this is right we should be interested to find out what happened one and a half years ago when this child was two and a half years old. I should understand it better if it had happened before the second child came but if it be true that the symptoms originated one and a half years ago we must know in what situation the woman was at that time and what has affected her. We shall find that she had to offer co-operation and could not, that she was afraid she would be subjugated and resisted and wanted to conquer.[20] But we must know.

> More careful examination, however, seemed to show that definite neurotic traits had been in existence many years, and had been accentuated since marriage. She herself indeed volunteered the information that she "had not been the girl she was since she had been married."

"Since marriage!" This is very interesting, because from our general experience we know there are three situations which are like test examinations [21] to show whether a person is socially interested or not: the social problem—how to behave to others; the occupation problem—how to be useful in work; the marriage problem—how to confer with a person of the other sex. These are the test examinations: how far a person is prepared for social relations. If her symptoms have been worse since marriage it is a sign that she was not *prepared* for marriage because she was too much interested in her own person.[22]

---

[20] Consistent with Adlerian theory, the crisis situation occurs when life demands an amount of cooperation that the person is unwilling to give because it would run counter to the dictates of the life style.

[21] There are more than three situations, but Adler here means three life tasks. Dreikurs and Mosak have pointed out that two more life tasks can be added to the traditional three, the task of getting along with oneself and the task of relating to a frame of reference outside the self, such as a deity. (Dreikurs R. & Mosak H. H. "The Tasks of Life II. The Fourth Task" The Individual Psychologist, Volume IV, No. 2, May 1967 and "The Life Tasks III. The Fifth Life Task" The Individual Psychologist, Volume V, No. 1, November 1967.

[22] This is another way of saying that she lacked social interest.

Now what of the family history? Many family histories I have read do not say very much. We Individual Psychologists are used to hearing of some situations and facts that involve the child in a way we can understand but we would reject all descriptions in which we are referred to heredity only, such as that an aunt was crazy or a grandmother a drunkard. These do not say anything. It does not contribute to our understanding. We are very interested in imperfect organs, if we are to grasp a case, because we find very often children out of a family tree where persons have suffered in some organs, and we may suspect that they suffer from some lack of validity in those organs; but mostly we do not get much information from these descriptions.

The family history showed signs of neurosis on both sides.

This is worth while, because we can see that the family history of the child had been a bad one. Neurotic means that the parents were fighting for things, to boss, to rule, to subjugate others, to utilise and to exploit others and so on, and therefore the children in such an atmosphere are really endangered. On this point, however, I have to say that although they are endangered, we are not sure that they must really suffer. They can overcome these dangers and get success and advantage out of them. But a certain probability gives us the right to expect that the danger is that the whole make-up and style of life will be in some way selfish.

At the same time it must be remembered that the informant on this matter was the patient, whose attitude to her parents, at least, was not without personal bias.

We want to see what her attitude was and this probably means that it was a hostile attitude to the parents; she has struggled against them.

For example she felt aggrieved that both her father and mother were only children—for, as she pointed out, this meant that she had no uncles or aunts and so could not receive presents as did other children.

This is a woman who is always expecting to be presented and here she betrays a good deal of her style of life. She is the type that wants to receive, not to give.[23] We understand that this type is in danger and must have difficulties in life, especially if she meets an ambitious man.

> *The father was a labourer. The mother was a hard-working woman who did everything to keep the home together. She avoided responsibility however, in one important particular. If her children needed correction, she preferred to leave that matter to her husband.*

This means that she did not feel strong enough, and utilised her husband for punishments, as happens very often in families. It is a bad thing for the children, because they begin to disesteem and ridicule the mother and to make a joke of her, because they see her express herself as a weak person, who cannot do the right thing.

> *This fact was unfortunate—since the latter was very sadistic.*

I do not think "sadistic" here is to be interpreted as meaning that he had sexual satisfaction when he slapped the children, but that he was rough and ruling and bossing and subjugated the children. Now we can understand that she has put her goal in the subjugation of others. I have known many cases where the child who has been beaten hard has gone round with the idea: "When I am grown up I will do the same with others—rule and boss them."[24] The father in his roughness has given this child a goal. What does superiority mean? What does it mean to be the most powerful person in the world? This poor girl, as a child who is always suppressed and maltreated, could have no other idea than that it is much better to be above and not down, to maltreat others and not to be maltreated. Now we see her from this standpoint and on this level.

---

[23] Here is another facet of the patient's life style. Not only does she feel surrounded by hostility and tries to subdue others, but she feels cheated by life because she has less people who will act as her servitors and providers.

[24] In imitation of the father. This means she will have an interest in being in the one-up or more powerful position, though she herself may feel subjectively weak even when she is using her power.

> *When he learnt from his wife that his children had misbehaved in any way—especially with reference to anything that touched his purse—for instance, if they wore out the soles of their boots quickly—he would beat them almost unmercifully.*

This is a point where we can learn something in regard to corporal punishment.[25]

> *The consequence was that the children lived in dread of their father, at the same time that for obvious reasons they did not confide in their mother.*

Where should they learn co-operation if neither with the father nor the mother? Some little degree of co-operation there must have been in this girl's mind, because she could get married. She may have learned it from other children, comrades perhaps, but not from father or mother.

> *Nevertheless she maintained that he was a good father, except on Saturday nights, when he frequently came home drunk.*

This would mean that she preferred the father. I am impressed, when I read this, with the idea that she was the eldest child. Mostly the eldest child, whether boy or girl, turns towards the father.[26] When another child comes relations with the mother are interrupted and the throne is vacant, which gives the father his chance. But this is only a guess and we have to prove it.

> *He would then strike his wife as well as his children and openly threaten to cut their throats.*

---

[25] Adler was entirely opposed to corporal punishment.

[26] This had also been noted by the editor. However, my explanation for it is different. The oldest child usually tries to imitate the parent who seems to be in the dominant position. This is usually the father in a patriarchal society such as ours. A common exception to this rule is the case of a first-born girl who tries to ally herself with the powerful father by behaving in a way that pleases him. See Shulman, B. H. "The Family Constellation in Personality Diagnosis." J. of Indiv. Psychol., Vol. 18, 35-47, May 1962 and also Ehrenwald, J. "Neurosis in the Family," New York: Hoeber, 1963, p. 12.

She imitates the father in her compulsion idea; to kill somebody with the knife—child, or husband. Did I not say that the father gave her the chance to put her goal of superiority in this way?

Notice that the father cursed only; he did not cut the throats of his children. Therefore I believe I am right in thinking that when she says she could kill somebody it is just a curse, an idea—"I could kill you!"

> *This latter point is possibly of interest in view of a similar symptom exhibited by A. Indeed in many respects her neurotic symptom formation tended towards an imitation of her father's characteristics.*

The writer, who is a doctor, goes on to say:

> *She was apt in the same way to hit her own children without adequate provocation.*

With this we do not agree. She has a provocation. She wants to be superior, as the father wanted to be superior. That is a provocation—she was provoked. If I want to boss I shall use my children, because they are the weaker ones and cannot hit back.

> *Though it is true she afterwards regretted her cruelty, ...*

This reminds me that we very often hear something said about regretting, feeling of guilt and so on. Now we Individual Psychologists are sceptical in this matter. We do not judge this regret and feeling of guilt very highly. We say it is absolutely empty and useless. After a child is beaten hard, the regret does not matter. It is too much. Either one of these two things would be enough—the regret or the hit—but both! I would resent it very much if somebody hit me and then regretted it. I have seen that this feeling of guilt is a trick so that we shall not see this cruel attitude in bossing others. It means: "I am a noble woman and I regret it." I believe modern society should be warned not to take very seriously this regret. We find it among problem children very often. They commit some act, cry, and ask pardon very much and then do it again. Why? Because, if they did not regret, but only continued doing it, they would be put out. Nobody could bear it always. They make a sort of hinterland where others will not interfere with them, they have a feeling that they are being smart children or people. So there is this woman, she is cruel and regrets it, but what does that matter? The facts are all the same.

> . . . this feeling had little or no power to prevent similar outbursts on a subsequent occasion.

We expected that, because it is a trick. Where you find the feeling of guilt it is in cases of melancholy and it is always a trick. It doesn't work. You see we guessed rightly.

> A was the second child and girl of a family of eight—four girls being followed by four boys.

In regard to second children, we know they are generally —though there are no rules, and we speak only of majorities —much more striving. It is like a race, and they want always to overcome the first child. The reason why I said I believed she was a first child was that she turned to the father, but there are circumstances in which the second child may do so, especially if she has been pampered and a third child comes and she is in a situation which draws her towards him.

We find second children striving to be first, there is a very good picture of this in the Bible picture of Jacob and Esau. It is very interesting, too, to see from statistics in America, that among juvenile delinquents, second children are in a majority. An enquiry into children of one and two years and younger has been started by Individual Psychologists and there is a big field, which can be used for some understanding of their whole style of life. There will be something good or something wrong about second children. It is like a race; they try to overcome the first. Perhaps it was so in this case, but we do not want to say more.

> As a child, she said, she had been on the whole happy-go-lucky, cheerful and healthy, . . .

If so, she had been in the centre of the stage and favoured. She was perhaps the favourite.

> ... very different from her eldest sister whom she described as being silent and reserved, characteristics which A interpreted as selfishness.

Now, surely, it is selfish to be reserved because it means to think of one's self. We can see that she had been lucky in her striving and the elder girl had the aspect of a defeated child and was overcome. We find this feature in her whole make up—how to overcome. She is able to succeed in her goal to be mother and father and to boss, in an easy way, because the elder sister has given way and been conquered.

> The parents seemed to have held a somewhat similar opinion, and treated their eldest child with special severity.[27]

Now the parents help her in her race, by suppressing the eldest child.

> She was frequently in trouble, and the severe beatings which she received from her father filled A with terror.

She had been scared because the eldest child had been beaten so severely.

> The rest of the family A regarded with considerable affection, with the exception significantly enough, of her eldest brother.

That is, the first boy, who when he came was probably worshipped and appreciated in a way she did not like and therefore, we can conclude—though we must really prove it —that her position in the family was endangered by this boy.

> As with her sister, so with him, she considered that he was selfish and inconsiderate, "so different from the rest of us, except, of course, T" (the eldest sister).

That she agreed with the other children means that she could rule them; they did not make difficulties. This boy and the eldest sister made difficulties and therefore she did not agree with them.

---

[27] Adler was not so wrong in his guess that Mrs. A. was an eldest child. Although she was born second, she overran the eldest and therefore could in some respects play the role of eldest.

> Personal History: *As already mentioned A had been a healthy child and prided herself on her robust health. From the age of fourteen to seventeen inclusive, however, she had some degree of goitre from which she subsequently recovered.*

We see here a certain organic imperfection, as we find very often among neurotic patients. How far this influenced her we could learn only from the first child, of whom we have not many remarks.

> *Though she had no return of the trouble, yet, from time to time in the course of treatment she had considerable difficulty in times of stress in getting her breath—a symptom which caused her considerable anxiety.*

This probably was not due to pressure of the thyroid, or it would have been recognised and treated. It probably was a psychological problem; she could not breathe, when she became emotional under the treatment, or it may have appeared when she was wishing to pose, or felt she was unjustly treated. All this may have affected her breathing, but it could have been seen clearly if the thyroid was causing pressure.

> *Her school attainments were quite good and she had at that time no difficulty in making friends.*

Do not forget that such persons, selfish from the beginning and striving to be in a favourable situation, do not lack all degrees of co-operation. Therefore, we are not astonished that she, who probably succeeded in the beginning and wanted to be ahead and lead the school, found it easier to make friends. Probably they were friends who were willing to submit to her but that is a point we could find out in an interview.

> *She left school at the age of fourteen, but continued to live at home for some months, going from there to daily work, which she enjoyed.*

In that case she probably fell on a good place, where she could express her opinion and perhaps also rule others.

> *But as soon as she entered domestic service away from home, new troubles began.*

THE DIAGNOSIS OF A LIFE-STYLE

Now domestic service means to *submit*, and this woman cannot submit. She cannot submit in any way that can be accepted as *co-operation*. She must be *ruling* and here we have a new proof. She is not prepared for a situation in which others are ruling. We find many girls who have to do domestic work and cannot submit. For instance, I remember a governess who, when the woman who employed her asked her to clean the cage of the parrot, said: "You should ask what I want to do this afternoon, and I will say that I would like to clean the cage of the parrot." Thus it appeared to be her own idea; she was *commanding*. You meet the same thing in the exercises of the army, where the soldier, after he is commanded, must repeat the command in such a way as if it were his own. "I shall go on this parade." You see the wisdom of that rule in the army.

> *Within a week of her arrival she was attacked by such bad carbuncles on her back that the doctor ordered her home again.*

I do not go so far as to say that those carbuncles were the result of her dislike, but it is a fact that if a person does not feel well in a certain place, something may happen. My daughter, who is a psychiatrist and has made researches into accidents found that half of them occur among persons who do not like the job in which they are working. When people are run over, fall down from certain places and hurt themselves, or touch something, it is as though they would say: "It is because my father forced me to go to this job, and I wanted another job." Half of all the accidents! Therefore, I am quite sure that things like carbuncles can occur if a person does not like a certain situation. I would not go further.

> *This she did with considerable trepidation because she knew that her eldest sister, who had once similarly returned, owing to illness, had had a very bad reception.*

She had learned how not to behave!

> *For a time, however, everything went well. But soon her father became openly dissatisfied at having to keep his daughter "eating her head off" as he put it. Matters came to a climax when, one morning as A entered the kitchen to*

> have breakfast, her father, without a word of warning, rushed at her with a shovel, obviously intending to hit her over the head.

It was in the morning, so he was not drunk!

> She rushed from the house in terror and hid from the family for the rest of the day. It is possibly of significance, in view of her later fear of coffins, undertakers and all matters relating to the subject of death, that she spent most of this time in the churchyard.

Now a new idea appears.[28] In a certain way we can see that the illness and the neurotic symptoms of this woman are an accusation against the father whether she knows it or not. We are studying the natural history, the biology, of behaviour. Now if we find one bone—such as this neurotic symptom represents—we can relate it to the father. The father is guilty and it is an accusation against him. She might put it in these words: "My father has tortured me so much that it is because of his treatment that I am as I am." Now the father had not been right, but does it follow that the daughter also must not be right? Is it really like cause and effect? Is she forced to be sick and to make mistakes because the father has made a mistake? The importance of this question is very great because that is what this woman, if we read her aright, is really saying—that because the father has made a mistake she also must do so. But there is no causality in mind; only the causality *she* has effected. She has made something into a reason which must not be a reason, and I have seen other children who have been tortured by their parents go through this compulsion neurosis. It is not like the causality we find among dead things [29] and, even among dead things, causality is now beginning to be doubted.

> In the evening, however, she was found by her mother who persuaded her to return home. Her father treated the incident as a joke, and laughed at her for "being such a silly."

---

[28] The case history has just described a traumatic incident. Adler denies that such incidents *must* cause psychic damage and suggests that the memory of a trauma can be used by a person as a justification for what he really wants to do anyway.

[29] meaning inorganic matter.

His daughter, however, did not treat the matter so lightly and vowed that she would never return home to live again, a resolution which she kept for a long time.

Another resolution she has made, as I said before: "I must never be in a situation where another person can rule me." In the childish fashion which we always find in neurotic patients, she knows only contradiction and antithesis: to rule or to be ruled. This is very interesting that among all the failures in life, and not only among neurotic persons, you will find that they know only contradiction. They call it sometimes "ambivalence" or "polarity" but always they are forming judgments of contradiction—down, above; good, bad; and so on; normal, not normal. In children and neurotic persons, and in the old Greek philosophy, you find always this looking for contradiction.

She has concluded, in this way, never to be ruled.

After this affair she went once more into domestic service and appears to have worked hard and diligently. She showed, however, a preference for rough work. Her dislike for doing "fiddly work" such as dusting, she distinctly stated to be due to her dread that she would break ornaments and so on.

What is in her mind is that she is a girl of strong health, who values strength and does not like housekeeping.[30] When we remember her contradiction towards the eldest boy, because a boy had been preferred, she probably did not want to be a woman at all. She disliked doing such things, being occupied with dusting and such little matters. This would explain why she was not prepared to be a married woman. This would be what I have called the [*masculine protest*]. In such a case if you force a person to do things she does not like, she tries to exaggerate. There is a certain anger and rage and exaggeration.

---

[30] Adler will explain this behavior by calling it a "masculine protest," because it is a refusal to imitate some aspects of feminine behavior. An explanation more coherent with the rest of the life style would be to say that her interest in dominating and controlling leads her to avoid work that requires a more delicate hand. I would have liked to ask her if she had ever actually broken any ornaments.

This fact is of interest as being the possible fore-runner of her later openly destructive wishes and feelings.[31]

That is a remark I had made.

At the age of eighteen she was engaged to a young man whom she appears to have dominated.

We find the writer of this case history has been on the same track as we have, and she describes this domineering symptom, when she points out that she dominated this man.

In course of time, however, she came to dislike him for what she considered his "stingy ways" and after two or three years, dramatically broke off the engagement by throwing the ring in his face.

That is not what we expect from a girl; we expect milder processes! [32]

She related, however, with pride, that he still maintained a somewhat dog-like devotion to her, and even at the time she came for treatment still continued to ask after her. In spite of this manifestation of devotion she never showed any regret with reference to her behaviour in the whole matter.

In this case she does not regret because there is no reason for her to do so.

During the War she entered a munition factory in a provincial town, and it was then she met the man who is now her husband.

We now remember this man. He is a cripple and you sometimes find among men and women who want to dominate, that they are very fond of cripples and people who are weak in some way—sometimes drunkards whom they want to save, and people of a lower social status than their own. I would warn people—girls especially, but also the men—against choosing in this way because *no person in love or marriage can safely be looked down on.* They will revolt as this man revolted.

---

[31] As the history will indicate, Mrs. A. began to behave in a more and more angry way, imitating her father.

[32] not from an angry girl!

> *He was quartered in hospital at the time, invalided home from the War. He fulfilled her ideal of a possible husband in two most important respects—he was tall and he was not a drunkard.*

We can understand that the father had been strong with his drunkenness, and the reason many persons, especially girls, are afraid of drunkards is that they cannot rule them. Drunkards and creeping things, like mice and insects, they fear sometimes. You find very often that this fright is because they cannot rule and they can be surprised. We can understand why she would resent a drunkard, but why she preferred a tall man we do not know. It may have been the remains of her admiration of the father, or she may have been tall or have thought it was more worth while to rule a tall man than a short one. This could be found out only by asking her.

> *It is also possible that his injuries appealed to her love of power—her wish to assume the dominant role was a notable trait in her character.*

The writer has taken the line which I explained. We would underline this and say her style of life was characterised by a very domineering and bossing attitude.

> *For a time all went well. But when her fiancé went to London, he then, for reasons best known to himself, wrote letters well calculated to rouse her jealousy.*

If we undersand that she wanted to rule him, to be alone with him and the centre of his attention, we know that jealousy is very near at hand. She has to look to it that she is not dethroned as she was when the other children came in the family, and when the boy came.

> *Unhappy and suspicious, A followed him to London, obtained work as a waitress in a restaurant, and did all in her power to hold her fiancé.*

You see how she is striving to keep him.

> *With this the attitude of the two lovers towards each other seems to have undergone a change. Not only did the woman assume the more active part in their relations. . . .*

We note this in proof of her meaning—she took the active part!

> ... but the man from being attentive and kindly, now became careless and inconsiderate.

We saw in the beginning that she had forced him to be careful. At this point we read he had become careless.

> They made appointments for which he either came late or did not keep at all. A became suspicious, tearful and "quite different from her former bright self."

She was afraid of losing her former ruling position.

> Matters came to a head when he failed for a second time to keep an appointment with her—she having in the meanwhile waited for him for hours in the cold and fog of a November night.

That is a hard thing, and there is no question the man also was not adapted for such a marriage. Any girl would be right to look upon such negligence as an injury. This girl could find no other way than the creation of a compulsion idea with which she could again conquer him.

> When she learned from him next day that he had not kept his appointment because he had gone out with some friends, she angrily told him she did not wish to see him again.

She would feel defeated. Perhaps we should be glad to get rid of such a partner, but this person does not *want* to be defeated. She *wants* to keep him.

> Her attempt to break off the engagement, however, did not take place—a fact for which she felt thankful when, three weeks later she discovered that she was pregnant.

Here is a good chance to speak of relations before marriage. It may seem in some cases to be an advantage, but I have found that it is a disadvantage and as doctors we should advise to wait. It always causes trouble.

> She felt desperate at this finding and entertained now for the first time definite suicidal feelings. Her fiancé endeavoured to comfort her and promised to marry her as soon

> *as possible* [33]—*which he did three or four weeks after. The question of her residence for the next few months now arose. She dreaded to return home because her father had said that he would have nothing to do with any of his daughters if they got into trouble. Though this threat proved to be unfounded, and she was allowed by her parents to return home, she felt very unhappy during this time.*

Really, she felt defeated.

> *Her misery was accentuated by the birth of a son: for both she and her husband had hoped for a daughter.*

This is something we should not expect. We should expect that if a child was coming they would hope for a son. Why they wanted a daughter could be explained only by these two persons. But perhaps if they had had a daughter, she would have been disappointed.

> *It may be pointed out in passing that A's desire for a daughter and subsequent disappointment were connected with her later hostility towards her sons.*

As we cannot control her statements without asking her, we must assume that she had disliked the man in her environment. Then her brother came. Probably, too, she was looking for the antithesis *man-woman,* because these neurotic people look on men and women as *opposite* sexes. You know the widespread notion—the *opposite* sex. If you exaggerate this you will get an opposition against the *opposite* sex, which is very often to be found, both in men and women, and especially among neurotic persons.

> *After this event she then returned to London to live in two rooms with her husband. Matters, however, went badly from the first. It is true that to begin with she got on well with her neighbours, but soon feelings of inferiority began to assert themselves. These seem to have been connected with a certain jealousy of her husband who was popular and well-liked generally. She interpreted passing words and looks of those around her as criticisms directed against herself.*

---

[33] What could not be achieved before by other methods can now be achieved by suicidal feelings. Now the man is willing to submit to her wishes and she has found a new way to dominate.

She looked on the neighbours probably, as subjects she could rule, and therefore, good relations never existed.

> As a conscious reaction formation against the sensation that she was despised, she not only avoided making friendships, "keeping herself to herself" as she described it, but she also used to sing hymns in a loud voice to show her neighbours firstly, that she was not afraid and, secondly, that she at any rate had been well brought up. Unfortunately her criticisms of her neighbours were not without justification, quarrels and drunken brawls not being infrequent. In addition she and her husband found constant cause for disagreement. The methods she employed to gain his sympathy were characteristic. Thus after a quarrel she would retire to bed and threaten to kill herself and the child unless matters improved.

You see how she wanted to use force!

> So matters continued, going from bad to worse until A's neurotic symptoms became so manifest that her husband took her to see a doctor. The diagnosis of nervous dyspepsia was made, and the recommendation given that all her teeth should be extracted.

I presume this was meant as a punishment; not as medical treatment! [34]

> After some hesitation she decided to take this advice and with this end in view went to hospital accompanied by a friend. The latter was then considerably annoyed when A after an hysterical outburst in front of the doctor and nurses, refused to have her mouth touched.

This suggests that she really understood the situation better!

> Not unnaturally this same friend refused to accompany her a second time to hospital. On the second occasion, therefore, A went alone, when it is noteworthy that, though nervous, she was able to have three or four teeth extracted without trouble. On the next occasion, however, matters did not go so smoothly. She had an hysterical outburst following the extraction of twelve teeth, due, she maintained, to the fact that she saw and felt the whole operation although under

---

[34] Naturally, Adler derides this method of treating nervous dyspepsia.

an anaesthetic. The phantastic nature of these "memories" was obvious. In accord also with her sadistic tendencies it is hardly surprising that these "remembrances" to which she had not infrequently referred, made a deep impression on her.

Now, imagine this woman: thirty years of age! They extracted, as far as I can count, sixteen teeth! I think a woman who had no "sadistic tendencies" would not look on this fact in a humorous spirit! It makes a deep impression. If you know what it means to a woman or a man to lose the first teeth, you will appreciate that this woman has lost sixteen. And she is jealous of her husband! She explained how she had suffered. I hope I am explaining it rightly, but this may have another explanation. This woman likes to explain how much she has suffered. Probably she had some dreams, as happens in narcosis and she tells these things to impress others how she has suffered.

I do not think we should speak of sadistic tendencies in the way that has become common in our time, because we should use it only when the person has a sexual gratification. If we call all forms of attack "sadism" everything disappears in darkness.

Shortly after this her second child was born.

We see that it was a time of distress when she was fighting hard for her superior position.

> *The fact that he was a boy caused her great disappointment—she had been quite certain that the infant would be a girl. The impotence of her wishes in the face of reality severely wounded her vanity—and from now on her neurotic tendency became more and more evident. The resentment she felt toward her infant was the obvious prelude to her later consciously felt wish to kill the child.*

You will remember that in speaking of the first symptoms and when they occurred, I said I could have understood it if it had been when the second child came, because her importance would weaken and become less, since she now has to share with two children and she wants to be the centre, not the children. She will feel resentment more strongly and a desire to kill.

> At the same time her pursuit by a drunken neighbour, who, with a knife in his hand threatened to take her life, gave her a reason for an exacerbation of her symptoms. It also gave her a reasonable excuse for refusing to stay in the house where they were living, although it was impossible to obtain any other room at the moment in the neighbourhood.

Now really this house had not been very well fitted for a bossing woman. The neighbours did not like her. In this case you can find also that a paranoiac symptom appears and you can see that in a certain way the manner in which this woman behaves is in the neighbourhood of paranoia—as if the others would pursue her and be interested in her and look at her. But even a compulsion neurosis reaches further and touches some symptoms which are generally described under another title. There are mixtures in this way.

> In addition—by this means she was able to leave her husband for a time, she and her children finding a temporary home with her mother-in-law, her husband remaining alone in London. The arrangement, however, did not prove happy.

The mother-in-law probably also did not submit!

> This position was partly due to the critical attitude of the mother-in-law towards her daughter-in-law, and partly to the fact that A felt hostile towards her mother-in-law from the start owing to the unfavourable comparisons which her husband was accustomed to draw between her and his mother.

The usual fact!

> By mutual consent, therefore, the arrangement was terminated and A and her children went to stay with her parents. From there she was recalled to London owing to the fact that her husband had had a "nervous breakdown" in her absence and wanted her to nurse him.

We do not know the husband. Perhaps he also wanted to dominate somebody.

> It seems improbable that it was only a coincidence that at the same time he had been able to find rooms for the family.

THE DIAGNOSIS OF A LIFE-STYLE

Probably he worked with nervous symptoms and wanted to impress her in this way by a "nervous breakdown." [35]

> *Shortly after her return to London she was overcome by the obsessive thoughts and feelings which gradually came to occupy her attention more and more—to the exclusion of almost all else. She dated this phase of her illness back to a terrifying dream of angels surrounding a coffin.*

This is the thought of death, but you see what it means. It affects the husband. *He* has to take care of her; so she has a dream of angels surrounding a coffin.

> *Of significance is her constant association of this dream with a picture at her old home at which she frequently gazed when pregnant with her first child.*

We understand that at this time she played with the idea of suicide. She looked round and the picture was there, and the other members of the family would be impressed. She would get the idea: "What would make me master of the game would be if the others were afraid that I would commit suicide."

The rest of the case-paper deals with treatment, which is not part of my lecture. I have simply wanted to show you the COHERENCE OF A LIFE-STYLE.[36]

---

[35] The husband and wife seem to have used "symptoms" as one of their ways of fighting each other.

[36] Adler does more than delineate a Life Style in this reading. He describes many of the dynamics of the neurosis itself. Let us review the points of General Diagnosis:
1. What produces the feeling of deficiency (the critical problem): her inability to rule the world around her, especially her husband and other "men" in her life.
2. The direction of striving: to overcome, control and keep her husband busy with her by having thoughts of suicide and other obsessive ideas.
3. Relationship of her striving to the "right degree of cooperation." It betrays a lack of social interest, excessive concern with her own power over others, an oppositional attitude and distrust of others. Human relations, for Mrs. A. are for the purpose of securing dominance or fighting against submission.

4. The lack of preparation: She lacks not courage, but training in cooperation. She has been trained in power relations by her father. Obviously, his aggressive power made him number one in the family. She is likely to equate cooperation with submission.
5. The evasive movement: Severe obsessive thoughts and other neurotic symptoms act as a "dragon." The symptoms are so troublesome that everything else must be postponed while one deals with the symptoms. One can't be bothered with other problems until one has first slain this dragon. See Shulman, B. H. and Mosak, H. H. Various purposes of symptoms, previously cited.
6. The arrangement of superiority: superiority is achieved in a painful way by little triumphs; as when the husband agrees to marry her after she threatens suicide, the husband finds another apartment, the former suitor displays his devotion, the husband has a breakdown and needs her, etc. (This is an unfortunate price to pay for such petty triumphs). As Adler says, "What would make me master of the game would be if the others were afraid that I would commit suicide."
7. Past history: the power contest in the home, between herself and her siblings and herself and father; which trained her to value conquest rather than cooperation.

To these points of General Diagnosis I would like to add additional items that are often useful:

8. Against whom is the neurosis directed? The answer here is obvious; it is against the husband and children mainly.
9. What is the Style of Life: It is the style of a complaining dictator. See Shulman, B. H. "A Comparison of Allport's and the Adlerian Concepts of Life Style." Individual Psychologist, 1965, 3, 14-21.
10. How well are the patient's maneuvers working? They work only at the price of neurosis and inability to function without suffering.
11. What is the patient's view of herself? Contrary to the way others see her, she sees herself as abused by her father, husband, by her children being male rather than female and so on. She considers herself a miserable unfortunate, fearful of others and suffering from unpleasant obsessive thoughts. She feels like a victim, while Adler sees her excessive concern with dominating, her hostility to others and her power contest with them.

The postscript by Hilda Weber shows how she responded to the therapist with a power contest at first and is a good example of how a patient may fight a therapist by becoming frightened or hostile whenever the therapist tries to bring up issues before the patient is willing.

POSTSCRIPT

Dr. ADLER broke off his consideration of Mrs. A's case at the stage in the recital of her life-history when a certain dream came to assume considerable importance in her life, but some account of the subsequent course of the case may be not without interest. Mrs. A presented herself for treatment eighteen months after the occurrence of the dream just mentioned. She was at that time in a state of great anxiety. Trembling, nervous, and terrified of strangers, she spoke with difficulty on any subject, while any attempt to follow up associations leading to matters of a personal nature threw her into such a state of agitation that for some time it seemed unlikely that she would continue treatment. She did not, however, attempt to leave.

She resisted all references to her childhood, owing, as it later appeared, to her sense of guilt with regard to certain childish games and practices of a definitely erotic nature. For a considerable period any allusion to her suicidal or homicidal tendencies was liable to arouse fear and hostility, and later the dread of insanity became prominent.

But in time, as she found that she was free to deal with any subject without fear of criticism from her physician, the severity of her own censorship diminished and she was able to give free vent to her repressed feelings. She thus learned to face her personality in all its aspects, both negative and positive, and so a notable change has taken place in her mental outlook. Her attitude to her family has grown more kindly and tolerant; lack of self-confidence, timidity, and avoidance of neighbours have been replaced by tendencies of an opposite nature, while added interest and enjoyment of life have made her altogether happier and more contented.

This change was, however, gradual, and the course of treatment has been subject to considerable fluctuation. Nevertheless after some months progress became marked.

The diminution in the strength of her homicidal impulses has been accompanied by a loss of her suicidal tendencies, with the apparently paradoxical result of a corresponding decrease in her fear of death.

Her love of order and cleanliness still remains, but is altogether less obsessional in character. Thus she keeps her home well, but if the children are a trifle noisy or untidy, she will remark: "Well, after all, with children, what else can one expect?" A very different attitude, this, from the state of irritation and fury into which she would formerly have been thrown under similar circumstances!

A change is also shown in her behaviour to her husband: warmer feelings have been substituted for frigidity, and cooperation rather than domination is the end desired.

The loss of any advantages gained by illness have been therefore amply compensated by the benefits obtained: homicidal and suicidal impulses have been replaced by a more courageous outlook; by love, interest, and zest in life.

HILDA WEBER